FLANNEL "Cookbooks for Guys" Anthology

By Tim Murphy

Copyright 2013
Shamrock Arrow Media

For information on Flannel John's Cookbooks for Guys, upcoming releases and merchandise visit www.flanneljohn.com

TABLE OF CONTENTS

APPETIZERS & SNACKS

BAKED BEANS

3 cans of pork and beans
3 pieces of bacon
½ of a large onion, chopped
½ cup of brown sugar
1/3 cup of molasses
1 teaspoon of mustard
Pinch of salt and pepper

Cook bacon and crumble into small pieces. Mix all ingredients in a 9" by 13" pan. Cover and bake at 250 degrees for 3 hours.

BAR CHEESE

2 pounds of Velveeta cheese
6 ounces of horseradish
8 drops of Tabasco sauce
1 cup of mayonnaise

Combine cheese, Tabasco sauce and horseradish in a double boiler. If you don't have a double boiler, put ingredients in a small pot and place in a larger pot half-filled with water. Once melted, remove from heat and add mayonnaise. Mix thoroughly. Pour into a container and let cool.

CAJUN WINGS

2 pounds of chicken wings
1 tablespoon of vegetable oil
1 teaspoon of crushed red pepper
2 teaspoons of Cajun seasoning
¾ teaspoon of corn flour
6 tablespoons of brown sugar
2 cups of orange juice
1½ cups of lemon juice

Combine vegetable oil, red pepper, Cajun seasoning, chili powder, corn flour and brown sugar in a bowl and mix well. Stir in orange and lemon juices. Place chicken wings in a dish and cover with mixture, holding back ½ cup. Cover the dish and place in refrigerator overnight. Remove from the refrigerator and place coated wings in a baking dish. Bake at 300 degrees for 20 to 25 minutes, basting every few minutes with the extra half cup of sauce.

CHILI DIP

8 ounces of cream cheese
1 can of chili (no beans)
½ cup of grated cheddar cheese

Place cream cheese in the bottom of a microwaveable baking dish. Cover with chili and top with grated cheese. Heat in the microwave on high for 3 minutes or until cheese melts.

FLORIDA KEYS DIP

8 ounces of cream cheese
1 cup of fresh lobster or crab meat
1 cup of sour cream
2 crushed cloves of garlic
1 chopped green onion
4 tablespoons of mayonnaise
1 teaspoon of lime juice
Salt and pepper to taste

Put ingredients in a blender. Serve dip with crackers or fresh vegetables.

GORP

Raisins
Dry roasted peanuts or almonds
Sunflower seeds, shelled
Rolled Oats
M&Ms, carob, chocolate or vanilla chips

Mix equal parts of each ingredient and store in a sealed container or plastic bag.

HANGOVER BARS

1 cup of Karo syrup
1 cup of sugar
1 cup of peanut butter
6 cups of Special K cereal
1 cup of chocolate, vanilla or butterscotch
    Chips (or a mixture of these flavors)

Mix syrup and sugar in a pan and bring to a boil. Remove from heat and add peanut butter and Special K. Press the mixture into a greased 9-inch by 9-inch pan. Melt chips of choice and pour over cereal mix. Consume after a night of over-indulging in strong drink.

HOMEMADE POTATO CHIPS

3 large potatoes
Vegetable oil
Salt

Slice potatoes paper thin to about one-sixteenth of an inch. Place slices in ice water until you are ready to fry. In a deep fryer or pan, heat oil to 375 degrees. Place 6 to 8 slices on paper towels to dry then slide slices one at a time into the oil. Fry 8 slices at a time until golden brown. Drain on paper towel and salt. You can also try celery or garlic salt.

JAPANESE CHICKEN WINGS

2 dozen chicken wings
1 cup pineapple juice
1 cup soy sauce
1 cup sugar
¼ cup water
¼ cup vegetable oil
2 cloves garlic, crushed
1 teaspoon ginger

Combine all ingredients in pan except chicken and ginger. Once thoroughly combined, add ginger and refrigerate overnight. Next day, pour off about 1 cup of liquid and place chicken in the pan. Bake uncovered at 350 degrees for 60 minutes. Baste wings with remaining liquid during baking.

MAN CANDY ROLL UPS

½ cup of sour cream
½ teaspoon of onion salt
½ pound of bacon, cooked and crumbled
1 package of crescent rolls (8 ounce size)

Mix sour cream, onion salt and bacon then spread on the rolls and roll them up. Bake at 375 degrees for 12 to 15 minutes.

MEDITERRANEAN GREEK BREAD

1 cup of mayonnaise
1 cup of mozzarella cheese
½ cup of butter
1 cup of sour cream
1 small can of sliced olives
4 chopped green onions (tops only)
1 large loaf of French bread

Split loaf of bread. Mix all ingredients and spread on bread. Bake at 375 degrees until the edges turn brown. This makes enough spread for 4 loaves.

SALAD DRESSING

¾ cup Miracle Whip or Mayonnaise
¼ cup ketchup

Whip together. Diced sweet pickle or relish is optional. For a richer flavor mix ingredients in a one-to-one ratio.

SAUSAGE BALLS

2 pounds of sausage (chopped or diced)
3 cups of Bisquick
1 large jar of Cheez Whiz

Mix all ingredients in a bowl. Form into 1-inch balls and bake at 350 degrees for 15 minutes.

STUFFED JALAPENOS

¼ pound of ground beef
12 popper-size jalapeños
1 small onion
1 pound bacon
14 ounces Monterey Jack with jalapeños
Cooking oil

Chop onion and brown in oil. Add hamburger, brown and drain. Grate cheese and mix with hamburger. Cut top of jalapeños and core out the seeds. Slit down to ¼ inch from bottom. Stuff with hamburger mixture. Wrap slice of bacon around popper. Stick with toothpick. Bake, broil or grill.

STUFFED MUSHROOMS

Mushrooms, fresh about 1 to 2 inches in size
5 tablespoons of bacon, crumbled or bits
3 green onions, chopped
8 ounces of softened cream cheese
½ cup of cheddar cheese

Wash mushrooms and remove stems. Place upside down on a cookie sheet. Chop stems. In a bowl mix stems, bacon, green onion and both cheeses. Spoon mixture into mushroom caps. Bake at 350 degrees for 15 minutes.

SWEDISH MEATBALLS

¾ cup of bread crumbs
½ pound of ground veal
2 pounds of ground beef
¼ pound of ground pork
2 eggs
3 teaspoons of salt
2 onions, chopped
¼ cup of parsley
Pepper to taste
Water

Add water to bread crumbs to form a damp paste. Mix with remaining ingredients. Refrigerate until cool. Form into 1½-inch balls and slowly brown in a skillet.

TRAIL HEAD JERKY SNACK

Jerky
Unsalted, roasted peanuts
Cashews
Raisins
Dates, chopped
Sunflower seeds
M&M's or Reese's Pieces
Dried bananas

Cut jerky into small bits and add equal amounts of other ingredients.

BREADS & MUFFINS

BACK COUNTRY BISCUITS

1¾ cups of flour
¾ teaspoon of salt
3 teaspoons of baking powder
½ cup of hard margarine
¾ cup of milk

Mix flour, salt and baking powder in a bowl. In a second bowl, blend margarine and milk. Now combine wet and dry ingredients and stir until well mixed. Press dough out on a floured counter. Cut biscuits into desired size. I use a soup can with the lid removed as a cutter. To make them bigger, I'll use a tuna fish can. Bake at 400 degrees until golden brown, approximately 10 minutes.

BEER BREAD

3 cups self-rising flour
3 tablespoons sugar
1 can of beer
3 tablespoons melted butter

Combine ingredients thoroughly and pour into a greased loaf pan. Bake at 350 degrees for 45 minutes or until golden brown. Brush or drizzle melted butter on top.

BEER MUFFINS

2 cups of Bisquick
2 tablespoons of sugar
1 cup of beer
1 cup of cheddar cheese (optional)

Mix all ingredients. Fill greased muffin cups 2/3 full of batter and let stand for 10 to 15 minutes. Bake at 375 degrees for 15 minutes. Makes a dozen muffins.

BREAK OF DAWN MUFFINS

2 eggs
½ cup of water
1/3 cup of milk
2 tablespoons of vegetable oil
1 package of peach cobbler mix
1 package of cornbread muffin mix

Combine eggs, water, milk and oil. Stir in mixes and blend well. Fill greased and floured muffin cups half way. Bake at 350 degrees for about 20 minutes or until muffins test done.

CORNBREAD

1 cup of cornmeal
1 cup of soy flour (or wheat flour)
2 teaspoons of baking powder
¼ cup of dry milk
¼ teaspoon of salt
2 eggs
1 cup of milk

Combine cornmeal, soy flour, baking powder, dry milk, salt and mix well. Add eggs and milk and mix well. Pour into a greased 8-inch by 8-inch pan. Bake at 400 degrees for 20 minutes.

GINGER BREAD

1¾ cups of flour
1½ teaspoons of baking powder
¼ teaspoon of soda
2 teaspoons of ginger
½ teaspoon of cinnamon
½ teaspoon of salt
1/3 cup of shortening or lard
½ cup and 1 tablespoon of sugar
1 egg
2/3 cup of molasses
¾ cup of buttermilk

Mix dry ingredients. Cream butter, add sugar then cream together. Add egg and molasses then flour and milk alternately. Bake in a greased, floured pan at 350 degrees for 50 minutes.

PUMPKIN BREAD

1½ teaspoons of salt
4 eggs
3½ cups of flour
1 cup of oil
2 teaspoons of baking soda
1 teaspoon of nutmeg
1 teaspoon of cinnamon
2 cups of pumpkin
3 cups of sugar
2/3 cup of water

Mix all ingredients thoroughly. Bake in a greased loaf pan at 350 degrees for 1 hour.

BREAKFAST

APPLE OATMEAL BREAKFAST BARS

1 cup of shredded raw apples packed into cup
1 teaspoon of grated orange or lemon rind
1½ cups of regular oats
2 tablespoons of oil
¾ cup of water
½ teaspoon of salt
¾ cup of chopped dates
¼ cup of chopped nuts
1½ teaspoons of vanilla

Blend ¾ cup of oats on high to turn into flour. Pour into bowl and add the remaining ingredients. Stir thoroughly. Press into a greased 8-inch by 8-inch baking dish. Bake at 375 degrees for 20 to 25 minutes. After cooling, cut into bars.

BAKED OATMEAL

½ cup of melted butter
1 cup of brown sugar
2 beaten eggs
3 cups of uncooked quick oatmeal
2 teaspoons of baking powder
1 teaspoon of salt
1 cup of milk

Mix all ingredients. Bake at 350 degrees for 30 minutes in a 9-inch by 9-inch pan.

BELGIAN POPPED WAFFLES

2 cups biscuit mix
1 egg
3 tablespoons oil
1¼ cups of club soda
    (Sierra Mist, 7-Up, etc)

Mix thoroughly. Pour into a pre-heated waffle iron or on griddle for pancake-style. Makes a half-dozen. Experiment with different carbonated beverages. Cherry Coke turned out pretty good.)

BREAKFAST BACON PIE

12 slices of bacon, fried and crumbled
1 cup shredded cheese, Swiss or cheddar
¼ cup chopped onion
1 cup Bisquick
1/8 teaspoon of pepper
4 eggs
2 cups milk
¼ teaspoon salt

Lightly grease pie plate. Sprinkle bacon, cheese and onion in pie plate. Beat remaining ingredients until smooth. Pour evenly into pie plate. Bake at 400 degrees for 35 minutes. Let stand for 5 minutes before cutting.

BREAKFAST SHAKE

2 scoops of low fat yogurt
½ banana
½ cup fresh fruit of choice
1 cup skim milk
2 ice cubes

Mix all ingredients in a blender, the battery-powered type for those non-electric camps. Or put into a jug and shake until your arms are exhausted.

BREAKFAST SPAM

12 ounce can of Spam
3 cups rice
8 eggs
Soy sauce

Cut Spam into ¼ inch slices. Brown both sides in skillet and set aside. Steam rice and set aside. Scramble 8 eggs in skillet. Put rice on plates, top with eggs and put Spam on the side. Sprinkle with soy sauce.

BROWNED BREAKFAST HASH

2 cups chopped cooked beef, chicken or ham
2 cups copped cooked potatoes
1½ onions, minced
2 tablespoons parsley
1 cup milk
Salt and pepper
Vegetable oil or Crisco

Mix all ingredients except milk. Place oil in a skillet over medium heat. When hot, spread mix evenly in skillet. Brown bottom of hash quickly, 10 to 15 minutes. Now add milk and mix. Cover and cook slowly until crisp, about 10 minutes.

CHOCOLATE CHIP PANCAKES

2 cups of Bisquick
1 cup of milk
2 eggs
½ cup of chocolate chips

Combine Bisquick, milk eggs and chocolate chips and mix well. Pour onto hot griddle and top with syrup or chocolate sauce. This recipe also works with vanilla and butterscotch chips.

CINNAMON MONKEY BREAD

3 cans refrigerated biscuits, cut into quarters
1 cup sugar
¾ cup butter
2 teaspoons cinnamon

Cook sugar, butter and cinnamon on low heat while cutting up biscuits into a non-stick Bundt pan. Pour mixture over the top and bake at 350 degrees for 30 minutes. Cover for first 10 minutes of baking with tin foil.

CRAB OMELETTE

½ cup of fresh crabmeat
½ cup of mushroom soup
4 eggs beaten
1 tablespoon of milk
Salt and pepper
Butter

Melt butter in a pan. Pour in beaten eggs. Cover and cook slowly. Heat crab and mushroom soup in a separate saucepan. Turn eggs over and place crab mixture on top and fold over. Cover and cook for 2 minutes. Salt and pepper to taste.

EGG CASSEROLE

8 eggs
2 cups milk
1 teaspoon salt
7 slices of bread, cubed
1 cup grated cheddar cheese
1 pound of cooked ham, sausage or bacon

Beat eggs well and mix with milk and salt. Stir in cubed bread and grated cheese. Cut or shred meat into small pieces and add them to mixture. Pour into a greased 8-inch by 10-inch dish and bake at 350 degrees for 45 minutes.

EGGNOG WAFFLES

2 cups biscuit mix (Bisquick)
¼ teaspoon nutmeg
1½ cups eggnog
2 tablespoons salad oil
1 egg

Mix all ingredients thoroughly until smooth. A rotary mixer may be helpful. Pour into waffle maker or onto a griddle for a pancake-style.

FARMHOUSE PANCAKES

1 cup of flour
2 tablespoons of sugar
½ teaspoon of baking soda
2 tablespoons of oil or melted butter
½ teaspoon of salt
1 cup of buttermilk (fresh or powdered)
1 egg, beaten

Mix flour, sugar, soda and salt. Whisk buttermilk, oil and egg together. Add to flour mixture and mix well. Be careful not to over-beat

FRENCH TOAST

2 cups milk
4 eggs
½ teaspoon salt
2 teaspoons cinnamon
Sliced bread

Beat four eggs thoroughly then mix all ingredients together. Dip bread into mixture until well coated. Fry on an oiled griddle or skillet until golden brown.

HAM & EGG SCRAMBLE

1 package frozen fried potatoes
2 cups cubed ham
1 egg per person
1 small onion
Butter or margarine
Salt, pepper or seasoning to taste

Fry potatoes in butter and add diced or chopped onion. Beat eggs and pour over potato mixture. After eggs are pretty well cooked, add ham and cook on low for 15 minutes.

HUEVOS RANCHEROS

2 tablespoons cooking oil
1 small green or red pepper, finely chopped
1 small onion chopped
1 clove garlic, minced (optional)
1 teaspoon of chili powder
8 ounces tomato sauce
1 pound tomatoes, chopped
6 eggs
1 package of tortillas
Salt and pepper

Heat cooking oil in a large skillet and sauté pepper, onion and garlic until mushy. Stir in chili powder, tomato sauce and tomatoes. Cook until bubbly. Lower heat and season with salt and pepper to taste. Drops eggs into hot sauce and simmer over low heat, covered, until eggs are firm. Serve eggs with tomato sauce and tortillas.

POTATO PANCAKES

4 cups mashed potatoes
1 tablespoon of flour

Mix potatoes and flour. Divide in half. On a floured surface, roll out each half to 1/8 inch thickness. Cut mixture with round cookie cutter (can with lid and bottom removed). Fry on un-greased pan until brown on both sides.

ROOKIE COOK FRENCH TOAST

2 cups milk
4 eggs
½ teaspoon salt
2 teaspoons cinnamon
Sliced bread

Beat four eggs thoroughly then mix all ingredients together. Dip bread into mixture until well-coasted. Fry on an oiled griddle or in fry pan until golden brown.

SEVEN-POUND BREAKFAST

2 pounds of tater tots
2 pounds of sausage or ham in cubes
1 pound of grated cheddar cheese
1 dozen eggs
1 cup of chopped onions
½ cup of milk
Salt and pepper to taste

Butter a 9-inch by 15-inch baking dish. Put tater tots, meat and cheese in the dish. Thoroughly mix eggs, milk, salt and pepper in a bowl and pour over tots, meat and cheese. Bake at 325 degrees for one hour. Serves 12 women or 6 men.

SPAM, EGGS & RICE

1 12-ounce can of Spam
3 cups rice
8 eggs
Soy sauce

Cut Spam into ¼ inch slices. Brown both sides in skillet and set aside. Steam rice and set aside. Scramble 8 eggs in skillet. Put rice on plates, top with eggs and put Spam on the side. Sprinkle with soy sauce.

SUNRISE WAFFLES

1 cup of flour
2 eggs
4 tablespoons melted butter
2 teaspoons baking powder
1 cup of milk

Beat egg yolks and add milk, butter and flour. Mix thoroughly. Add egg whites. This will fill iron 3 or 4 times.

BURGERS, DOGS & MORE

BACON CHEESE BARBECUE DOGS

8 hot dogs
8 hot dog buns
8 slices of cheddar cheese
8 slices of bacon
½ cup of barbecue sauce
1 red onion, diced

Place bacon in a deep skillet. Cook over medium-high heat until browned and drain on paper towels.
In a separate pan or on a barbecue, grill hot dogs cook browned and fully cooked, or until done to your taste. Lightly toast or grill hot dog buns. Now place a slice of cheese and bacon on each roll. Add a hot dog, top each with 1 tablespoon barbeque sauce and red onion.

BARBECUE NOT-SO-SLOPPY JOE BURGER

        1 pound of ground beef
        1 cup chopped onion
        1 cup of ketchup
        2 tablespoons mustard
        1 teaspoon of salt
        1 teaspoon of sugar
        1 teaspoon of vinegar

Brown ground beef and onions. Stir in remaining ingredients. Cover and simmer 30 minutes. Optional method: form 4 to 6 patties with all ingredients and toss them on the grill.

BARBECUE PORK BURGERS

        2 pounds of ground pork
        ¼ cup of fresh bread crumbs
        1 cup of barbecue sauce
        6 burger buns
        Salt and pepper to taste

Mix ground pork with bread crumbs and ½ cup of sauce to make six patties. Grill burgers on medium high heat, basting burgers often with remaining sauce. Takes about ten minutes to cook, five minutes per side.

BEER BARREL BRATS

4 bratwursts
2 bottles of beer
8 slices of pumpernickel bread
Spicy brown mustard
Horseradish
Oil

Slowly simmer brats in a large skillet with beer for 10 to 15 minutes. Place on an oiled grill or in a second oiled skillet on low heat. Once they're browned, slice each brat down the middle and make a sandwich with the pumpernickel bread. Spread with spicy brown mustard and/or horseradish.

BLEU CHEESE BURGERS

2 pounds of ground beef
8 ounces crumbled blue cheese
2 tablespoons onion powder
2 tablespoons garlic powder
2 tablespoons soy sauce
2 teaspoons salt
4 slices Swiss cheese
4 hamburger buns

Combine ground beef, blue cheese onion powder, garlic powder, soy sauce and salt in a bowl. Mix well to make 4 large patties. Grill patties on high heat for about 8 minutes per side or until well done. Top with Swiss cheese

DEVIL DOGS

1 package of hot dogs
1 can of jalapeno peppers
1 package of fresh carrots
1 onion, coarsely chopped
Corn chips

Cut hot dogs into bite-sized chunks. Cut carrots into ¼-inch thick slices. Put all ingredients in a slow cooker and heat until juice is reduced by half. Serve with corn chips.

FIRST MATE'S CLAM BURGERS

1 pint of razor clam necks, uncooked
2 eggs
1 teaspoon of parsley flakes
2½ teaspoons of onion flakes
4 drops of Tabasco or hot sauce of choice
2 teaspoons of Worcestershire sauce
¼ teaspoon of pepper
1 teaspoon of biscuit mix
3 soda crackers
Butter
Hamburger buns

Grind clams. Beat eggs and add parsley flakes, dried onion flakes, Tabasco, Worcestershire sauce, pepper and biscuit mix. Crumble soda crackers and add all of these ingredients to ground, mixed clams and mix well. Form small patties and fry in ½ to 1 inch of oil in a pan. Brown both sides well. Check center for doneness. Serve on buttered, toasted hamburger buns.

GRILLED CHEESE & PEAR SANDWICH

    Sour Dough Bread
    Butter or Margarine
    Sliced Sharp Cheddar
    Sliced Havarti
    Mayonnaise
    Creamy Horse Radish Sauce
    Bacon Bits
    French's French Fried Onions
    Pear Jam or preserves
    (peach or apricot work too)

For each sandwich butter one side of each slice of bread. On the other, spread one with a mixture of mayonnaise and horseradish sauce and one with the pear jam. Then between the 2 slices, add a slice of each cheese, bacon bits and French fried onions. Close and fry in pan until golden brown and cheese has melted.

GRILLED CHEESE PIZZA BURGER

8 slices of bread
¾ cup pizza sauce (or Prego sauce)
8 slices of mozzarella
24 slices of pepperoni
2 tablespoons Crisco
Toppings of choice

Spread 1 teaspoon of sauce on each piece of bread. Place slice of cheese on 4 bread slices and 6 slices of pepperoni. Add other four slices of cheese and bread. Melt 1 tablespoon of Crisco in skillet on medium heat and add sandwiches. Grill 2 to 4 minutes until golden brown. Add remaining Crisco, let melt and turn sandwiches to grill other side.

HOBO HAMBURGER

1 pound of hamburger
1 onion
2 carrots
2 potatoes
Salt and pepper to taste

Make burger patties and place on aluminum foil. Thinly slice onions, carrots and potatoes and place on top of meat. Salt and pepper to taste. Fold foil into a pocket and fold edges over. Cook on grill or open fire.

NEWPORT CRAB BURGERS

8 hamburger buns
2 cups of crab meat
1 cup of shredded sharp cheddar cheese
1 to 1½ cups of mayonnaise
1 teaspoon of lemon juice
Garlic powder to taste

Mix all ingredients. Place mixture on hamburger buns and bake in the oven at 350 degrees until the cheese is bubbly.

ONION BURGERS

1 pound of ground beef
1 cup of chopped celery
1 can of condensed French Onion soup
¼ cup of water
¼ cup of catsup
1 teaspoon of Worcestershire sauce
1 teaspoon of yellow mustard
¼ teaspoon of pepper
Hamburger buns

Brown ground beef and celery in a pan and pour off fat. Add remaining ingredients and cook over low heat for 12 to 15 minutes. Scoop onto buns.

PIZZA DOGS

4 hot dogs
4 hot dog buns, split
½ cup of marinara sauce
4 ounces of mozzarella, shredded
¼ cup of diced pepperoni

Cook the hot dogs on grill or in a skillet for 5 to 8 minutes, according to the package directions. Place a hot dog in each bun and, dividing evenly, top with the warmed marinara, pepperoni and mozzarella. Grill, bake or broil until the mozzarella has melted and browned, about 2 minutes.

PORCELAIN PALACE MINI-BURGERS

1½ pounds of ground beef
1 egg
1 instant onion soup mix
½ cup diced onion
2 teaspoons water

Mix and press into a cookie sheet. Poke holes in meat placing diced onions in holes. Bake at 400 degrees for 10 minutes. Cut into squares use dinner rolls for buns.

QUESADILLA BURGER

6 ounces of ground beef
2 ounces of salsa
1 ounce shredded cheddar cheese
1 burger bun
Hot sauce (optional)

Grill the burger and place on the bun. Top with a few drops of hot sauce, salsa and cheese.

REUBEN SLIDERS

1½ cups of corned beef, chopped
1 cup of sauerkraut
½ cup of shredded Swiss cheese
½ cup of Thousand Island dressing
1 loaf of thin-sliced cocktail rye

In a bowl combine corned beef, drained sauerkraut, shredded Swiss cheese and Thousand Island dressing. Mix well. Place mini-sandwiches on a baking sheet and bake at 375 degrees for 10 to 12 minutes or until cheese is melted.

SLOPPY JOE

1 pound of ground beef
1 package French's Sloppy Joe mix
6 ounces of tomato paste
10 ounce can of chicken & rice soup
1 can water
1 chopped onion
1 bell pepper

Brown hamburger or deer meat. Drain the fat. Add sloppy Joe mix, tomato paste, soup and water. Simmer for 30 minutes. Serve on bread or buns.

TAILGATE HOT DOGS

8 hot dog buns
8 hot dogs
½ cup of butter
2 tablespoons of mustard
2 tablespoons of Parmesan cheese
1 tablespoon finely chopped green pepper
1 tablespoon of chopped onion
1 16-ounce can of pork and beans

Cream butter and add in mustard, cheese, onion and green pepper. Open split buns, place on foil and spread mixture. Cut dogs in half and place on buns. Top with beans. Bake at 350 degrees for 12 to 15 minutes.

TUNA BURGERS

1 can of tuna fish
1 egg
½ cup of cracker crumbs
¼ cup of milk
¼ teaspoon of onion flakes
¼ teaspoon of oregano
Salt and pepper to taste
Cheddar cheese
Tomato slices
Lettuce
Oil

Mix fish, egg, cracker crumbs, milk, onion, oregano, salt and pepper then form into patties. Fry in skillet. Top with cheese, tomato and lettuce and serve on buttered, toasted hamburger buns.

TURKEY BURGERS

1 pound of fresh ground turkey
¼ cup of chili sauce
1 teaspoon of chicken flavor bouillon powder

Combine all ingredients and shape into patties and grill. Serve on toasted hamburger buns.

ULTIMATE GRILLED CHEESE

3 ounces of softened cream cheese
¾ cup mayonnaise
1 cup shredded cheddar cheese
1 cup shredded mozzarella cheese
½ teaspoon garlic powder
1/8 teaspoon seasoning salt
10 slices of Italian bread (½ inch thick)
2 tablespoons butter

In a bowl, mix cream cheese and mayonnaise until smooth. Stir in cheese, garlic powder and seasoning salt. Spread 5 slices of bread with cheese mixture and top with remaining bread. Butter outside of sandwich and toast in a large pan or skillet for about 4 minutes a side or until golden brown.

WALKING TACOS

1 small bag of corn chips (Fritos work best)
½ pound of ground beef, cooked
1 onion chopped
2 tomatoes, chopped
1 cup of salsa
1½ cups of shredded cheese, taco blend

Open bag of chips slightly and crush chips in bag. Now open bag completely and mix in the ingredients as you like. Sprinkle in hot sauce for the extra kick.

CHILI

BEEF JERKY CHILI

½ cup of chopped bacon
1 onion, chopped
2 cloves of garlic, minced
2 cups beef broth
4 chili peppers, chopped
2 tablespoons chili powder
2 tablespoons light brown sugar
1½ tablespoons of cumin
5 cups fresh tomatoes, peeled & chopped
½ tablespoon pepper
2½ cups of beef jerky, chopped
2½ cups kidney or pinto beans, cooked

Cook bacon in deep pot or Dutch oven until fat is released, but not crisp. Add onion and garlic and cook until tender. Add in chili peppers, tomatoes and broth. Cook until tomatoes are soft, 15 to 20 minutes. Now combine chili powder, brown sugar, cumin and pepper and then add to pot. Stir in the beef jerky. Simmer or low boil for 45 minutes. Add beans and boil for about 5 minutes.

CHICKEN CHILI

1 pound of boneless skinless chicken, diced
3 cups of chicken broth or stock
1½ cups of diced tomatoes with juice
2 jalapenos chopped with seeds removed
15 ounces of pinto or red beans (canned)
15 ounces of black beans (canned)
2 tablespoons of oil
1 medium onion, chopped
2 large cloves of garlic, minced
4 teaspoons of chili powder
1 tablespoon of ground cumin
2 teaspoons of oregano
Lime and cilantro (optional)

Drain and rinse beans. Sauté onion and garlic in oil. Add chicken and cook on medium until meat is no longer pink. Stir in chili powder, cumin and oregano. Add chicken stock, tomatoes, jalapenos, salt, pepper and beans. Simmer uncovered over low to medium heat for 15 minutes.

CHILI MEAT LOAF

2 pounds of ground beef
1 can of chili with beans (15 to 16 ounces)
2 eggs, lightly beaten
1 medium onion, chopped

Mix ingredients and place into a greased shallow baking dish. Bake at 350 degrees for 90 minutes.

HALF-TIME CHILI

2 pounds of ground beef
1 cup of onion, chopped
1 clove of garlic, minced
1½ teaspoons of salt
1 teaspoon of paprika
1 teaspoon of oregano
1/3 cup of chili powder
15 ounces of tomato sauce
16 ounces of pinto beans
2 cups of water

Brown ground beef with onion, garlic and seasonings. Add tomato sauce, water and pinto beans. Simmer for at least one hour. Start making it just before kick-off and it will be ready at half-time.

VEGETARIAN CHILI

30 ounces of canned red kidney beans
½ cup of dried lentils
1 tablespoon of olive oil
1 onion, chopped and peeled
1 red pepper chopped with no seeds
1½ cloves of garlic crushed
14 ounces of tomatoes
1 teaspoon of paprika
2 tablespoons of chili powder
Salt and black pepper
¼ teaspoon of sugar

Simmer lentils and beans in water for 40 to 45 minutes, until tender. Heat oil in a large pan and sauté onion and pepper for 10 minutes. Add in garlic and cook for 1 to 2 minutes and then add tomatoes. Drain the beans and lentils, reserving the liquid. Add beans and lentils to the tomato mixture with the chili powder and paprika. Simmer for 15 minutes, pouring in the bean water as needed for consistency. Season and add sugar.

WINTER'S NIGHT CHILI

1 pound of meat of your choice
2 cans of stewed tomatoes
4 cans of pinto chili beans
1 green pepper
1 onion, diced
1 teaspoon of chili powder
Salt and pepper

Brown meat and sprinkle with salt, pepper and chili powder. Combine with beans and stewed tomatoes. Chop onion and green pepper and stir-fry in meat grease until tender. Pour into bean mixture and simmer for 30 minutes.

DESSERT

APPLE COBBLER

1 stick of margarine
1 cup of flour
2/3 cup of sugar
2 cans of apple pie filling

Take margarine, sugar and flour and mix well. Pour apple pie filling into a 9-inch by 13-inch pan. Crumble above mixture over the top and bake at 350 degrees for 1 hour or until golden brown. Recipe also works with cherry pie filling.

APPLE CRISP

5 cups of sliced apples
¾ cup of flour
1 teaspoon of cinnamon
1 cup of brown sugar
¾ cup of rolled oats
½ cup of butter

Arrange apples in a buttered pan. Combine sugar, flour, oats and cinnamon. Cut in butter until crumbly. Press over apples. Bake at 350 degrees for about 45 minutes.

ARMY NAVY DOUGHNUTS

5 cups flour
2 cups sugar
½ teaspoon salt
1 teaspoon of nutmeg
2 eggs
5 teaspoons baking powder
1¼ cups of milk
1 teaspoon melted butter

Sift dry ingredients. Combine eggs, butter and milk. Add dry ingredients. Mix well. Shape into a ball and knead. Roll out on floured surface and cut with doughnut cutter. Place in deep fryer or in a deep skillet. Makes four dozen. This recipe was used to serve tens of thousands of allied troops throughout Europe during World War I.

BLACK BOTTOM BARNACLE CUPCAKES

8 ounces of cream cheese
½ cup of sugar
1 lightly beaten egg
6 ounces of chocolate chips
1 devil's food cake mix

Beat cream cheese, sugar and egg until creamy then fold in chocolate chips. Prepare cake mix as directed and fill cupcakes to one-third full. Add a heaping spoonful of the cream cheese mixture and cover with cake mix to two-thirds full. Bake at 350 degrees for 20 to 25 minutes.

BUCKEYES

1 package of graham crackers, crushed
2¾ cups of powdered sugar
1 cup of peanut butter (crunchy or smooth)
1 cup of butter, melted
Chocolate or chocolate chips, melted

Combine crumbs and sugar. Melt butter and peanut butter then add to crumb mixture. Form into balls about 1½-inches in diameter. Chill, dip into melted chocolate and chill again.

FIVE-MINUTE KEY LIME PIE

1 prepared graham cracker pie crust
12 ounces of key lime yogurt
1 small package of lime gelatin
¼ cup of boiling water
8 ounces of whipped topping

In a large bowl, dissolve gelatin in boiling water. Stir in yogurt with a whisk. Fold in whipped topping. Spread into the crust and refrigerate overnight.

KAHLUA BOWL CAKE

1 box of chocolate cake mix
1 pint of sour cream
¼ cup of Kahlua
2 eggs
1/3 cup of vegetable oil
6 ounces of chocolate chips

Mix the dry cake mix thoroughly with the other ingredients. Because brands differ, follow baking directions on the box.

OREO BALLS

1 package of Oreos
8 ounces of cream cheese
7 ounces of Bakers Dipping Chocolate
   (microwaveable)
Popsicle sticks or skewers

Crush Oreo cookies. Add cream cheese and roll into 1½-inch balls. Insert sticks into balls and dip into melted chocolate. Freeze or refrigerate until hard. Dip balls a second time and place back in the refrigerator. Serve "down markers" on green florist foam to look like turf.

SEA MONSTER COOKIES

1 cup of butter or margarine
1 pound of brown sugar
2 cups of sugar
6 eggs
1½ teaspoons of vanilla extract
1½ teaspoons of syrup
4 teaspoons of baking soda
1½ pounds of peanut butter
9 cups of uncooked rolled oats
1 pound of M&Ms
6 ounces of chocolate chips

Mix ingredients in the order listed. Drop tablespoons of the mixture on a greased cookie sheet. Flatten a bit. Bake at 350 degrees for 12 minutes.

PECAN PIE

3 eggs, slightly beaten
1 cup of light or dark syrup
1 cup of sugar
4 tablespoons of melted butter
1 teaspoon of vanilla
1½ cups of pecan halves
9-inch pie shell, unbaked

In a bowl mix eggs, syrup, sugar, butter and vanilla until well blended. Stir in pecan halves then pour into pie shell. Bake at 350 degrees for 50 to 55 minutes. Test for doneness with a knife. Insert it into the center and if it comes out clean, it's ready.

POTATO CHIP COOKIES

2 cups of flour
1 cup of margarine
½ cup of sugar
1 teaspoon of vanilla
½ cup of chopped pecans
¾ cup of crushed plain potato chips
   (unsalted if possible)

Cream margarine, sugar and vanilla together. Mix potato chips, pecans and flour together. Now combine all ingredients. Roll into balls and flatten with the bottom of a glass dipped in sugar. Bake at 350 degrees for 10 to 12 minutes.

TIRED HUNTER COOKIES

¼ cup of brown sugar
½ cup of margarine (softened)
1 cup of flour
1 teaspoon of vanilla

Mix all ingredients and form into 1-inch balls then place on a cookie sheet. Bake at 350 degrees for 10 minutes.

DINNER

ALOHA CHICKEN

2 pounds of chicken breasts and thighs
¾ cup sugar
2 eggs, beaten
1 cup of flour
1½ cups of ketchup
¼ cup crushed pineapple
½ cup vinegar
1 teaspoon of salt
1 teaspoon of soy sauce
Garlic salt to taste
Rice (optional, steamed as side dish)

Wash and drain chicken. Lightly sprinkle with garlic salt. Let stand 5 to 10 minutes. Dip chicken in beaten eggs then coat with flour. Fry until browned then put in a baking pan. In a saucepan combine remaining ingredients and bring to a boil. Pour over chicken and bake at 350 degrees for 50 minutes. Serve with rice pouring any extra sauce over rice.

BARBARY COAST PORK CHOPS

4 boneless pork chops, ¼-inch thick
1 tablespoon of olive oil
1 clove of garlic, minced
2 tablespoons of oil
4 tablespoons of dry cooking sherry
4 tablespoons of soy sauce
2 tablespoons of brown sugar
2 tablespoons of cornstarch
2 tablespoons of water

Heat olive oil in skillet. Brown chops on both sides then set aside. Sauté garlic until lightly brown. Combine oil, sherry, soy sauce and brown sugar in a bowl until sugar is completely dissolved. Place chops back in skillet and pour mixture over them. Cover tightly and simmer over low heat until chops are cooked through and tender. If needed, add a little water to keep sauce from cooking down. Turn once. Removed from skillet. Combine cornstarch and water until smooth. Add to skillet mixture and stir thoroughly. Cook until thickened and pour over chops.

BARBECUED BEEF

4 pound beef roast
1 cup of ketchup
1 cup of barbecue sauce
2 cups chopped celery
2 tablespoons vinegar
2 tablespoons brown sugar
2 tablespoons Worcestershire sauce
1 teaspoon of chili powder
1 teaspoon of garlic powder
1 teaspoon of salt

Bake at 300 degrees for 4 to 5 hours. Shred beef or venison with fork and serve on rolls, buns or bread.

BEEF & RICE

1 pound ground round or lean hamburger
2 cans cream on onion soup
1 package of dry onion soup mix
1 cup of uncooked rice

Mix all ingredients and bake in a covered dish at 350 degrees for 60 minutes.

BEEF STEW WITH DUMPLINGS

24 ounce can of beef stew
10 ounce can of tomato soup
1 soup can water
1 cup Bisquick
1/3 cup water

In a saucepan combine stew, soup and water. Bring to a boil. Mix Bisquick and 1/3 cup water and drop by spoonfuls into boiling stew. Cook uncovered on low heat for about 10 minutes (stove or grill). Cover and cook for 10 more minutes.

BEER CAN CHICKEN

4½ pounds of chicken
3 tablespoons of oil (preferably olive oil)
1 half can of beer, room temperature
1 tablespoon of kosher salt or sea salt
1 tablespoon of dried thyme
1 tablespoon of black pepper

Rub the chicken with oil. Mix salt, pepper, thyme and sprinkle over chicken. Fire up the grill. When it reaches temperature, put the half empty can of beer on the grill, set up for indirect heat. Put chicken over the can so it is sitting upright, with the can in the cavity. Cover the grill. After one hour, check the chicken and refresh coals if needed. Using a meat thermometer, check every 15 minutes until the thickest part of the thigh reaches 160 to 165 degrees.

BOSTON HARBOR CHICKEN

3 frozen, skinless chicken breasts
1 package of onion soup mix
1 can of cranberry sauce jelly

Place frozen chicken in a crock pot. Pour dry soup mix and cranberry sauce on top. Put on lid and bake on medium heat for 3½ hours.

CAMP POTLUCK

1 chicken bouillon cube
¾ cup instant rice
1 package dry onion soup mix
3 cups water
8 ounces of soup vegetables or beans
   (dry or dehydrated works too)
5 ounces chicken, diced or shredded
¼ teaspoon hot sauce (optional)

Bring water and bouillon cube to a boil. Add remaining ingredients, continuing to stir until rice is cooked.

CAPTAIN'S TABLE ROAST

3 pound roast (beef, pork or deer)
2 cups of fresh brewed coffee
2 cans of cream of mushroom soup
1 package of dry onion soup mix
Salt and pepper

Flour and brown meat in a skillet. Put roast in a crock pot with remaining ingredients. Cook for 8 hours. This recipe is very effective for tough meat.

CHICKEN & RICE

2 cup cooked rice
8 ounces of diced chicken
1 cup crushed pineapple in its own juice
1 cup celery, thinly sliced
1 medium green pepper, diced
4 ounces shredded cheddar cheese
4 tablespoons mayonnaise
Salt and pepper to taste

Combine all ingredients except 2 ounces of cheese and mix well. Put in a casserole dish. Sprinkle remaining cheese over top. Bake at 350 degrees for 30 minutes.

CRISPY CORN CHICKEN

1 Fryer chicken in parts
4 cups corn flakes
½ cup evaporated milk
½ cup butter
1 teaspoon salt
1/8 teaspoon pepper

Crush corn flakes into crumbs and mix with salt and pepper. Dip chicken pieces in milk and roll in seasoned crumbs. Place chicken pieces skin side up in a single layer in pan. Drizzle with melted butter. Bake at 350 degrees for 60 minutes.

CHICKEN PARMESAN

3 pounds of chicken pieces
1 cup cornflake crumbs
   (or crushed corn flakes)
½ cup grated Parmesan cheese
¾ cup Miracle Whip

Combine corn flake crumbs and cheese. Coat chicken pieces with the Miracle Whip and then coat with crumb and cheese mixture. Put in dish and bake at 350 degrees for 60 minutes.

DAKOTA HILLS HOT DISH

2 pounds of ground beef
1 onion, diced
5 medium potatoes, cubed
1 large can of pork and beans
1 large can of tomatoes

Brown beef and onion in a skillet. Mix all ingredients in a baking dish. Potatoes can be cooked a little to speed the baking process. Bake at 350 degrees for 1 hour.

GREEK CHICKEN

1 chicken, cut up
5 potatoes
Garlic salt
Salt
Pepper
Oregano leaves
Lemon

Put chicken in big pot or Dutch oven. Season with salt, pepper, garlic salt and oregano. Peel potatoes and cut into quarters, putting them around chicken. Pour in 1½ cups of water, cover and put in oven at 350 degrees for 1 hour. Remove cover, squeeze on lemon juice, cook until brown.

HAM FRIED RICE

6 slices of bacon
½ onion, chopped
6 carrots, sliced and diced
3 celery stalks, sliced and diced
2 cups of cubed ham
2 scrambled eggs
2 cups of cooked rice

Fry bacon, remove and crumble. In the drippings, sauté onion until tender then add carrots, celery and ham. Cover and cook until tender. Stir in rice. Add bacon and scrambled eggs a few minutes before serving.

HONEY BARBECUE CHICKEN

3 pounds of chicken
3 tablespoons of honey
3 tablespoons of mustard
1 tablespoon of sesame seeds

Barbecue chicken on the grill or bake in the oven. Mix honey, mustard and sesame seeds. Ten minutes before taking off the heat, brush the chicken with the mixture.

HUNTERS DELIGHT

1 pound sliced bacon
1½ pounds of raw ham, cubed
1 large can tomato puree
1 large can of whole kernel corn
1 can of lima beans
1 can of mushrooms
1 package spaghetti
2 large onions

Cut bacon slices in half and fry. Fry cubed ham in bacon fat. Fry sliced onion until golden brown. Cook spaghetti as to package directions. Combine all ingredients. Bake at 350 degrees for 60 to 75 minutes. After eating a large portion, call a cardiologist!

ISLAND TERIYAKI STEAK

1½ pounds of top sirloin steak
½ cup of soy sauce
¼ cup of brown sugar
2 tablespoons of olive oil
1 teaspoon of dry ginger
½ teaspoon of MSG
¼ teaspoon of pepper
2 cloves of minced garlic

Combine all ingredients, except the meat, and mix well. Cut the steak into 1-inch strips about ¼ inch thick. Add sauce to the meat and stir well to thoroughly coat. Marinade for two hours. Place meat on skewers then bake, barbecue or grill.

LASAGNA

1½ cups of water
1 large jar of spaghetti sauce
16 ounces ricotta cheese
10 ounces mozzarella cheese
½ cup Parmesan cheese
½ pound of hamburger or venison
Lasagna noodles

Mix water, sauce and browned meat. Spoon a layer into a baking dish. Now cover with an overlapping layer of noodles. Next spread half the ricotta and mozzarella over noodles. Sprinkle with Parmesan and add another layer of sauce. Repeat the layers. Top with noodles and pour remaining sauce evenly and sprinkle with Parmesan. Cover with foil and place dish on a baking sheet. Bake at 350 degrees for 60 minutes. Remove foil and add a final layer of mozzarella and bake 10 minutes.

LIGHTHOUSE KEEPER'S CASSEROLE

3½ pounds of peeled shrimp
1 pound of crabmeat
6 cups of cooked rice
1 quart of mayonnaise
3 cups of chopped onion
3 cups of chopped celery
1 chopped bell pepper
6 tablespoons of Worcestershire sauce
2 tablespoons of salt
1 tablespoon of black pepper

Place ingredients in a pan and cover with foil. Cook at 350 degrees for 35 minutes. Remove foil for the last 5 minutes.

MEATLOAF

2 pounds of ground beef
1 pound of ground pork
2 cups tomatoes, chopped
2 eggs
1 cup of sweet cream
¼ onion, minced
Salt and pepper

Mix thoroughly and form into a loaf. Bake at 350 degrees for 90 minutes.

MEAT LOAF ITALIAN

2 pounds of lean ground beef
2 cups dry stuffing cubes
2 eggs
1 cup of milk
½ cup onion, minced
1 teaspoon of Italian seasoning
1 tablespoon of garlic, minced
1 tablespoon of Worcestershire sauce
1 tablespoon of steak sauce

Combine all ingredients in a large bowl. Put mixture in a loaf pan and bake at 350 degrees for 80 to 90 minutes. Use a meat thermometer to check internal temp. When the dial reads, "beef medium" it's done. Brown meat and drain. Add taco seasoning, water, corn, green pepper and tomato sauce and simmer for a few minutes. Put in an 8-inch baking dish. Make muffin mix according to instructions on package. Add ½ cup of onions. Top mixture in pan with muffin mixture. Bake at 350 degrees for 20 minutes (uncovered). Remove and add cheese and the remainder of canned onions. Bake 3 minutes.

MERMAID HAIR PASTA

2 cans of chicken broth
¼ pound of fresh, cleaned shrimp
12 mushrooms chopped into quarters
1 sliced green onion
Angel hair pasta

Bring chicken broth to a boil the drop mushrooms in. Gently boil for 5 minutes. Add in the cleaned shrimp and boil for 3 minutes. Add in green onion and boil for another minute. Strain ingredients and add them into the pasta and toss. Pour broth over everything for desired flavor.

PACIFIC STEAK

1 cup of soy sauce
1 cup of sherry
½ cup of peanut oil
3 small garlic cloves, minced
½ teaspoon of ground ginger
2 steaks

Blend first five ingredients together. Place steaks in fridge and marinate in the mixture for at least 6 hours, turning steaks after 3 hours. When ready to grill or fry, cook for 4 to 6 minutes per side.

POOR MAN'S STEAK

2 pounds of hamburger
1 cup of cracker crumbs
1 cup of milk
1 teaspoon of salt
¼ teaspoon of pepper
1 chopped onion
Flour
Oil (or butter)
1 cup of mushroom soup

Mix all ingredients together, except flour and oil. in the shape of a loaf. Chill overnight. Cut into slices and dip into flour then brown on both sides in a skillet. Place in a roasting pan or baking dish and cover with the mushroom soup and a little water. Bake at 350 degrees for 90 minutes.

PORK CHOP CASSEROLE

6 pork chops
4 potatoes
2 cans of green beans
2 cans of cream of mushroom soup

Brown pork chops in a skillet then place them in the bottom of a baking dish. Slice potatoes thick, place on top of the pork chops. Layer green beans and top with soup. Bake at 375 degrees for 1 hour.

PORK CHOPS

6 thick pork chops
1 large onion, thinly sliced
8 ounces of sliced water chestnuts
1 can of mushroom soup
1 can of French fried onions
3 ounces of sliced mushrooms

Brown pork chops, blot and paper towels and drain. Put chops in a large baking dish and layer with sliced onion, mushrooms and water chestnuts. Pour mushroom soup over everything. Top with French fried onions. Cover and bake at 325 degrees for 45 to 55 minutes.

POT ROAST

3½ pound roast; beef, veal or pork
1 can of condensed French onion soup
¼ cup of water
3 tablespoons of flour
Shortening

In a heavy pan brown the meat in a little shortening. Pour off fat and add soup. Cover and cook over low heat for 2½ to 3 hours. Stir occasionally. Gradually blend water into flour until smooth and slowly stir into sauce. Cook and stir until thickened.

PORK & APPLE MEAT LOAF

1½ pounds ground beef
½ pound ground pork
1 cup of applesauce
4 ounces of onion, diced
1 cup of bread crumbs
1 egg lightly beaten
3 tablespoons ketchup
2 teaspoons salt
¼ teaspoon pepper

Mix ingredients and form into a loaf pan. Bake 2 hours at 350 degrees.

ROUND STEAK WITH GRAVY

2 to 2½ pounds of round steak
1 package of onion soup mix
¼ cup water
1 can of condensed cream of mushroom soup

Cut steak into 5 to 6 pieces. Place in slow cooking pot or slow cooker. Add dry on onion soup mix, water and condensed mushroom soup. Cover and cook on low 6 to 8 hours.

SHEPEHERD'S PIE

1 pound of ground beef
¼ cup of chopped onion
¼ cup of chopped green pepper
1 can of condensed vegetable soup
¼ teaspoon of salt
¼ teaspoon of crushed thyme leaves
2¼ cups of mashed potatoes
Garlic salt to taste (optional)

Brown beef and cook onion and green pepper. Pour off fat and stir in soup, salt and thyme. Pour into a baking dish and spoon potatoes around the edge. Bake at 400 degrees for 25 minutes.

SOUTHERN STYLE FRIED CHICKEN

2 chickens (cut into 8 pieces each)
2 cups flour
1 cup of milk
1 teaspoon of salt
½ teaspoon ground pepper
½ cup butter
2 eggs

Mix milk, salt, pepper and well-beaten eggs in a bowl. Melt butter in skillet over high heat. Dip chicken pieces into milk mixture, coat with flour until completely dry and place in skillet. Turn continually until pieces are golden brown.

TACOS FROM SCRATCH

1 pound of ground beef
1 large onion, chopped
1 can of kidney beans
2 cans tomato sauce
1 tablespoon of chili powder
1 package taco seasoning (optional)
Taco shells
Salt and pepper
Lettuce, diced tomatoes, grated cheese,
Olives and sour cream for toppings

Brown ground beef and add chopped onion. Drain kidney beans, mash and add to meat and chopped onion. Add tomato sauce, chili powder, salt and pepper. Cook until thick. Spoon into shells and add toppings.

SAFE HARBOR SEAFOOD CASSEROLE

2 cans of tuna, shrimp, salmon or crab
2 cans of cream of mushroom soup
2 cans of cashew nuts
2 cups of water
2 cups of chopped celery
2 teaspoons of chopped onion
2 cans of chow mein noodles

Break up seafood. Mix two cans of soup with water. Mix all ingredients except the noodles. Put in ½ can of noodles. Bake at 350 degrees for 35 minutes. Take out of oven and top with remaining noodles. Wait 10 minutes and serve.

TEXAS GOULASH

2 pounds ground beef
1 can of tomatoes
2 cups uncooked macaroni or pasta
½ package chili mix
1 onion, chopped
1 can of whole kernel corn
1 can beef broth (or bullion and water)
1 tablespoon of sugar
½ cup cheese
Salt, pepper, garlic and oregano to taste

Brown ground beef and onion. Add remaining ingredients and mix well. Place in crock-pot on a low setting for 3½ hours. Add cheese when goulash is done.

TUNA NOODLE CASSEROLE

1 can of peas
1 can of tuna fish
1 can cream of mushroom soup
¼ cup diced celery
8 ounces of noodles
1 cup cubed cheddar cheese
Butter, Salt & Pepper

Cook noodles in boiling, salted water. Mix ingredients. Put in a medium buttered casserole dish. Bake at 350 degrees for 30 to 40 minutes or until lightly brown.

DRINKS

BREW-IT-YOURSELF ROOT BEER

2 cups sugar
½ bottle root beer extract
1 teaspoon of dry yeast
½ cup warm water
1 to 2 cups water

Pour 3 tablespoons or ½ bottle of root beer extract over 2 cups sugar and add enough water to dissolve. Add 1 teaspoon of dry yeast to ½ cup warm water to dissolve. Add both mixtures together and pour into gallon jug. Top off jug with warm water and let sit for 6 hours, uncapped. Tighten lid and refrigerate. After 24 hours it's ready to drink. The longer it sets, the better it tastes.

CAPTAIN'S GROG

2 ounces of dark rum
½ ounce of fresh lime juice
1 teaspoon of brown sugar
4 ounces of hot water
1 orange slice
1 cinnamon stick

Mix rum. Lime juice, brown sugar and hot water in a tankard. Garnish with orange slice and cinnamon stick.

CITRUS COVE ICED TEA

4 cups of boiling water
4 tea bags
6 cups of cold water
½ cup of orange juice
½ cup of lemon juice
Sugar to taste

Pour boiling water over tea bags and steep for 5 minutes. Remove tea bags and add cold water and juices. Chill thoroughly then add sugar to taste.

FIRESIDE COFFEE

1 cup of hot chocolate mix
1 cup of non-dairy creamer
½ cup instant coffee
½ teaspoon cinnamon
¼ teaspoon nutmeg
½ to ¾ cup sugar

Mix hot chocolate, creamer, coffee, cinnamon and nutmeg in a blender. Add in sugar and blend well. Drop in 3 to 4 heaping teaspoons per mug and pour in hot water.

ICE BOWL HOT BUTTERED RUM

1½ cup of dark rum
2½ cups of boiling water
4 tablespoons of butter
4 teaspoons of sugar
4 cinnamon sticks
Nutmeg

Stir sugar and rum together with a cinnamon stick until sugar has dissolved. Add water and butter. Pour into four mugs, dust with nutmeg and place a cinnamon stick in each one.

NAVAL GROG

1 ounce of light rum
1 ounce of dark rum
1 ounce of Grand Marnier
1 ounce of grapefruit juice
1½ ounce of orange juice
1½ ounce of pineapple juice

Pour liquors into an ice-filled glass. Add juices and shake.

PINK LEMONADE MILKSHAKE

3 cups milk
10 scoops vanilla ice cream
1½ cups of frozen pink lemonade
        concentrate

Mix together in a blender. Works with regular lemonade too.

SPICED APPLE CIDER

½ gallon of apple cider
½ cup of packed brown sugar
14 whole allspice
14 whole cloves
3 cinnamon sticks

Pour all ingredients into a large saucepan. Slowly heat to a boil, and then reduce heat to a simmer for 15 minutes. Remove from heat and strain.

FISH

ALMOND COD

2 pounds of Pacific cod
½ cup of flour
1 teaspoon of salt
¼ cup of slivered almonds
½ cup of melted butter
¼ cup of lemon juice
1 teaspoon of grated lemon peel
¼ cup of chopped green onion

Cut fish into bite size pieces. Coat a serving dish with non-stick spray. Drop fish into the flour and salt mixture and place in dish in a single layer. Pour butter, lemon juice and peel over fish. Bake at 350 degrees for 20 to 25 minutes. Sprinkle with roasted slivered almonds and chopped green onion.

CATFISH

Catfish fillets
Green onions
1 package of hollandaise sauce mix
Soy sauce
Butter or margarine.

Marinate catfish fillets in soy sauce for at least 2 hours. Grill or bake the fish. Pour Hollandaise sauce over fish. Sauté green onions in butter or margarine then sprinkle over the fish and sauce.

BAKED HALIBUT

4 tablespoons of olive oil
2 tablespoons of fresh lemon juice
2 6-ounce halibut fillets
Salt and pepper

Whisk together 2 tablespoons of the oil with lemon juice. Place halibut on a rimmed baking sheet. Sprinkle with salt and pepper. Drizzle with oil and lemon mixture. Bake at 425 degrees for 12 to 15 minutes, or just until opaque in the center.

BEER BATTER FISH

4 to 6 fish fillets
2 eggs, separated
¾ cup of beer (DON'T use dark beer!)
1 cup of flour
½ teaspoon salt
½ teaspoon paprika (optional)
2 tablespoons melted butter, cooled

Beat egg yolks until thick, gradually mix in beer. Add salt, flour, paprika and melted butter. Stir mixture until smooth. Beat egg whites until stiff and fold into batter, mix thoroughly. Wipe fish dry before dipping in batter. Fry in pan or deep fryer.

CREOLE TUNA

1 small can of tuna fish
2 tablespoons of butter
2 tablespoons of flour
2 tablespoons of chopped green pepper
1½ cups of milk
1 small tomato cut, peeled and copped
Salt and pepper to taste

Melt butter in a pan and add chopped pepper and tomato. Cook for 3 minutes then add flour and mix well. Add milk and stir until smooth. Add flaked tuna and cook for 10 minutes.

FRIED FISH

2 pounds of fish fillets
1 teaspoon of hot sauce
3 eggs, beaten
1½ cups of cornmeal
Cooking oil
Salt and pepper to taste

Rub fish with hot sauce, salt and pepper. Set aside in fridge for one hour. Cut fillets into chunks, dip into egg and roll in cornmeal. Fry quickly in oil for 2 to 3 minutes or until golden brown.

GREAT LAKES FISH IN SESAME BUTTER

2 pounds of walleye or northern pike
½ cup of melted butter
4 tablespoons of lemon juice
6 tablespoons of toasted sesame seeds
Salt and pepper
Worcestershire sauce

Arrange fish in a shallow, buttered baking dish. Season with salt and pepper and brush with butter. Bake at 350 degrees for 20 minutes. Heat remaining butter until lightly browned. Add lemon juice and a dash of Worcestershire sauce. Stir in sesame seeds. Spoon over baked fish when hot.

HONEY FRIED WALLEYE

6 large walleye fillets
¾ cup of vegetable oil
1 egg, lightly beaten
1 teaspoon of honey
1½ cups of crushed soda crackers
½ cup of flour
½ teaspoon of salt
½ teaspoon of pepper

Dry fillets with a paper towel. Heat oil is a skillet. Mix egg and honey. Dip fillets into the mixture of crackers, flour, salt and pepper. Pressing crumbs firmly into fillets. Fry for 2 to 3 minutes on each side.

MILLE LAC'S FISH STEW

5 pounds of walleye (or similar fish)
3 quarts of water
2 cans of tomatoes
3 chopped onions
3 potatoes, diced
4 hard boiled eggs, diced
4 strips of bacon, diced
½ stick of butter
1 large can of tomato paste
1 tablespoon of Worcestershire sauce
Tabasco to taste

Cover fish with water and boil until tender. Remove fish, add all the ingredients and simmer for one hour. Bone the cooked fish and add to stew for the last five minutes of cooking.

NORTHWEST CITRUS SALMON

1 orange
4 6-ounce salmon fillets
½ cup of soy sauce
¼ cup of sliced red onion
¼ cup of olive oil
2 minced garlic cloves
2 teaspoons of minced ginger root
¼ teaspoon of salt
1/8 teaspoon of pepper

Grate ½ teaspoon of orange peel and squeeze juice from orange; place in a resealable plastic bag. Add salmon, soy sauce, onion, oil, garlic and ginger; seal bag and shake to thoroughly coat. Refrigerate for 60 minutes. Drain and discard marinade. Place salmon on a baking sheet. Broil 6 inches from the heat for 10-12 minutes or until fish flakes easily with a fork. Salt and pepper to taste.

SKILLET FRIED TROUT

2 one-pound trout fillets, cleaned
2 ounces of butter
1½ cups of all-purpose flour
Salt and pepper

Season flour with salt and pepper. Roll trout in the flour mixture. Heat butter in the pan. Fry trout for 5 minutes on both sides until golden brown. If fish looks translucent or raw, it is not finished cooking. It should flake with a fork.

SOLE OF A PIRATE

1 pound of boneless, skinless sole, flounder
   or Whitefish about ¼ inch thick (4 pieces)
½ cup of chopped onion
½ teaspoon of minced garlic
14 ounces of diced tomatoes
1 teaspoon of drained capers
4 peppercorns
Hot pepper sauce
Vegetable oil or spray

Rinse fish and pat dry. Oil a large skillet and place over medium to high heat. Add onion and garlic and cook until tender. Stir in remaining ingredients and bring to a boil. Place fish on top and return to a boil. Reduce heat, cover and simmer for 5 minutes or until fish flakes easily with a fork. Remove peppercorns before serving.

SEAFOOD

BEER BOILED SHRIMP

2 pounds of cleaned, large raw shrimp
24-ounces of beer
2 tablespoons of crab boil seasoning
Pepper, lemon wedges and cocktail sauce

In a large pot bring beer and seasoning to a boil. Dump in shrimp and cover. Return to a boil and then simmer for five minutes. Turn off heat and leave shrimp in the pot for three minutes. Drain shrimp and serve with lemon wedges and cocktail sauce.

CALIFORNIA CRAB CAKES

1 egg
¾ cup of water
1 teaspoon of parsley flakes
½ teaspoon of prepared mustard
1 envelope of potato pancake mix
2 tablespoons of mayonnaise
7 ounces of crabmeat, drained and flaked
½ cup of fine, dry bread crumbs
3 tablespoons of butter

In a bowl mix egg, water, parsley, mustard and potato pancake mix. Stir with fork until blended. Let batter rest for 10 minutes. Add mayonnaise and crabmeat. For into 8 to 12 patties and dip in bread crumbs. Melt butter in skillet and brown cakes, about 4 to 5 minutes on each side.

CAROLINA CRAB

1 pound chunk of blue crab meat
½ cup of butter or margarine (melted)
1 tablespoon of vinegar
1 teaspoon of tarragon

Place crab in baking dish. Combine butter and vinegar, pour over crab. Sprinkle with tarragon. Broil until lightly browned, 10 to 15 minutes.

CLAM CHOWDER

3 dozen clams in shells
3 cups of clam broth
4 slices of bacon
4 tablespoons of melted butter
2½ cups of raw, diced potatoes
4 cups of milk
2 tablespoons of flour
2 medium onions
Salt and pepper to taste
Water

Open clams and drain the liquid through a cheese cloth. Grind clams. Fry up onions and bacon until brown. Combine clams, potatoes, bacon and onions. Add enough water to cook potatoes and clams. When finished, add clam liquid, milk and seasonings. Make a paste of melted butter and flour to thicken the mixture. Add butter, salt and pepper to taste.

CRAB SCAMPI

3 cups of crab meat or legs
1 green onion, chopped
1 green pepper, chopped
Olives, slice
Mushrooms, sliced
1 cup of butter (or margarine)
¼ cup of olive oil
Salt, pepper and garlic salt to taste

Melt butter and oil in skillet. Add ingredients and simmer until thoroughly heated. Serve over rice.

CRAWFISH CASSEROLE

2 cups of rice
1 pound of crawfish tails
1 stick of butter
1 chopped bell pepper
1 chopped onion
1 can of cream of mushroom soup
1 can of tomatoes with chili peppers, diced
8 ounces of cheddar cheese

Cook rice. Sauté vegetables in butter. Add tomatoes and crawfish and simmer for 10 minutes. Combine all ingredients in a casserole dish. Bake at 325 degrees for 40 minutes.

CRISPY BACON OYSTERS

12 ounces of drained oysters
10 slices of bacon cut in half
2 tablespoons of parsley
Salt and pepper

Place oyster on a piece of bacon and sprinkle with parsley, salt and pepper. Wrap bacon around oyster and secure with a toothpick. Repeat. Broil 8 minutes on one side, flip and broil 5 minutes on the other side.

NEW ENGLAND CLAM CHOWDER

¾ cup of chopped celery
¾ cup of chopped onion
1 tablespoon of butter
2 quarts of milk
Roux
8 ounces of clam juice
8 ounces of chopped clams
1 pound of cooked and diced potatoes
Salt and pepper to taste
¼ teaspoon of MSG

Sauté celery and onions in butter until tender. Add milk and bring to a simmer. Thicken slightly with roux and simmer for 15 minutes. Add remaining ingredients and simmer for an additional 15 minutes. Season to taste.

SEAFOOD ALASKAN

2 tablespoons of butter
2 tablespoons of flour
2 tablespoons of sherry
1 cup of cream
3 tablespoons of ketchup
2 teaspoons of Worcestershire sauce
½ pound of shrimp (cleaned and peeled)
½ pound of crab meat
Paprika
Cayenne pepper
Salt and pepper

Melt butter in a pan. Stir in flour until well-blended. Stir in cream slowly and once sauce is thick add ketchup and Worcestershire sauce. Now add in shrimp and crab and stir until well heated. Season with salt, pepper, paprika and cayenne pepper. Just before removing from heat, stir in sherry.

TIPSY SHRIMP

2 pounds of large prawns, shelled
2 ounces of dry Vermouth
2 lemons
1 ounce of butter
1 ounce of olive oil
1 garlic clove, crushed
½ teaspoon of ground black pepper
¼ teaspoon of salt

Pour olive oil into a skillet. Once it's simmering add shrimp and cook until golden brown. Reduce heat and add butter, garlic, salt and pepper. When well-blended, raise the heat and add the juice from both lemons and Vermouth and cook for one minute while continually stirring.

SIDES DISHES

APPLESAUCE FROM SCRATCH

8 apples peeled, cored and sliced
½ cup water
½ cup brown sugar
1 teaspoon of cinnamon

Heat apples and water in a deep pan for 5 to 10 minutes, stirring occasionally. Mix in the remaining ingredients. Heat until boiling and stir for 1 minute.

FIVE-CUP FRUIT SALAD

1 cup of pineapple bits, drained
1 cup of mandarin oranges, drained
1 cup of miniature marshmallows
1 cup of shredded coconut
1 cup of sour cream

Combine all ingredients and refrigerate overnight.

GREEN BEAN CASSEROLE

1 can of green beans
1 can of cream of mushroom soup
1 cup of grated cheese
16 Ritz crackers, crushed

Drain green beans and spread in a casserole dish. Now pour on the soup, sprinkle the cheese and top with cracker crumbs. Bake at 350 degrees for 30 minutes.

GREEN BEANS & MUSHROOMS

1½ cups of cooked green beans
1 tablespoon of butter
1 small finely chopped onion
2 ounces of mushrooms (canned or fresh)
1 teaspoon of instant beef bouillon
½ teaspoon of seasoning of choice

Prepare and drain beans. Melt butter in a small pan over low heat. Stir in onion and cook slowly until it is translucent. Add remaining ingredients, cover and bring to a boil. Add beans and cook uncovered for 1 to 2 minutes until beans are heated.

HOME-BAKED MAC & CHEESE

1½ cups of uncooked elbow macaroni
¼ cup of margarine or butter
1 small onion, chopped
½ teaspoon of salt
¼ teaspoon of pepper
1¾ cups of milk
¼ cup of flour
8 ounces of American cheese, cubed

Cook macaroni until tender. Drain and set aside. Cook and stir margarine, onion, salt and pepper over medium heat until onion is slightly tender. Blend in flour. Add milk, the cook over low heat stirring constantly until mixture is smooth and bubbly. Remove from heat and stir in cheese until melted.

HUSH PUPPIES

1 pound of corn meal
1 egg
1 tablespoon of baking powder
1 tablespoon of sugar
1 cup of buttermilk
Pinch of salt

Mix ingredients together, adding a little water of too dry. Form into balls. Cook in skillet or deep fat fryer at 350 degrees.

ONION ROASTED POTATOES

2 pounds of potatoes cut into chunks
1 envelope of dried onion soup mix
1/3 cup of oil (I prefer olive oil)

Mix oil and soup together in a Ziploc bag. Add in potatoes and shake to coat. Place potatoes on a cookie sheet and bake at 450 degrees for 40 minutes. Stir occasionally.

PASTA SALAD

1 package of tri-colored pasta
1 small bottle of Italian dressing
1 package of Italian dressing mix
1 sliced medium cucumber
1 cup of cherry tomatoes
1 can of large olives (6 ounces)
1 avocado, diced

Cook pasta, drain and rinse in cold water. Add dry dressing, cucumber, tomatoes and avocado to the pasta. Stir in ½ bottle of dressing and add olives.

POTATO CAKES

6 potatoes
½ cup of milk
1 cup of flour
2 teaspoons of salt
2 eggs
Shortening, oil or lard

Grate potatoes medium fine. Combine with salt, milk eggs and flour. Drop by spoonfuls into hot shortening or oil and flatten. Brown both sides.

SHRIMP & RICE SALAD

1½ cups of salad shrimp
3 cups of cooked rice
½ cups of sliced pimento olives
1 bunch of thinly sliced green onions
½ teaspoon of salt
¼ teaspoon of pepper
4 tablespoons of mayonnaise

Mix all ingredients together and chill for 2 hours.

STUFFED PEPPERS

1 can of chili (with no beans)
4 bell peppers
1 can of corn (drained)
Tortilla chips
Hot sauce (optional)

Cut the tops of the peppers and remove the insides. Boil in water for 12 to 15 minutes and drain. In a pan combine chili and corn and heat until cooked. Fill peppers with the mixture and hot sauce. Serve peppers with chips.

SUMMER SALAD

3 tomatoes
2 cucumbers
2 celery stalks
2 green onions
¼ cup of mayonnaise
Salt and pepper

Cut tomatoes into wedges. Slice cucumbers, celery and onions. Mix vegies together with mayonnaise. Salt and pepper to taste.

THREE BEAN SALAD

1 can of kidney beans
1 can of garbanzo beans
1 can of green beans
1 small red onion, chopped
½ cup of Italian dressing

Mix all ingredients and refrigerate for at least 2 hours.

WALDORF SALAD

4 cups of chopped apples
¾ cup of raisins
½ cup of pecan pieces
½ cup of mayonnaise

Combine all ingredients and refrigerate until you are
ready to serve.

SOUP & STEW

BEAN & BACON SOUP

1 pound of beans
4 slices of chopped bacon
1 chopped onion
2 stalks of celery, chopped
3 quarts of water
½ tablespoon of sugar
Salt and pepper

Soak beans overnight in water. Fry bacon until it's crisp, remove and drain. Add beans, bacon water, onion, celery and sugar. Simmer for about 3 hours.

BEER, CHEESE & BACON SOUP

3 slices of bacon, in pieces
½ cup of green onion, chopped
2 tablespoons of flour
1 can of cream of chicken soup
8 ounces of shredded Cheddar cheese
12 ounces of beer
1 cup of milk

Fry bacon until slightly crisp. Add onion and sauté until tender. Remove from heat and stir in flour. Add soup and heat until boiling. Stir in cheese until melted. Add beer and milk until foam disappears and soup is hot. Do not boil.

BROCCOLI SOUP

10 ounces of frozen, chopped broccoli
1¼ cups of water
1 cup of milk
½ cup of sharp cheddar cheese
½ cup smoked cheddar cheese
2½ teaspoons of chicken bouillon
Pinch of white pepper

Put water and broccoli in a pan and cook until broccoli is tender. Add in milk, bouillon and pepper. Heat until soup is back to a simmer. Add in cheese and stir continuously.

CHEDDAR CHEESE SOUP

½ cup butter or margarine
6 tablespoons flour
1 quart of milk
1 teaspoon of salt
2 cups shredded sharp cheddar cheese
½ cup of celery, diced
½ cup of green pepper, diced
½ cup of onion, diced
½ cup of carrots, diced
1 pint of chicken stock or broth

Combine flour, milk, cheese and salt and make a thick sauce. Sauté` celery, green peppers, onions and carrots in butter. Add chicken broth and cook until hot and vegetables are crunchy, add to cheese sauce. Stir thoroughly

CHICKEN & RICE SOUP

6 chicken legs
3 stalks of sliced celery
3 sliced carrots
5 sliced mushrooms
1 chopped onion
1 teaspoon of salt
1 tablespoon of soy sauce
2 cloves of garlic, chopped
½ cup of rice
Italian seasoning
Basil
Water

Cook chicken, celery, carrots, onion and salt in a large pot of water for one hour. Removed chicken from the bone and drop it in the pot with soy sauce, garlic, mushrooms, rice and spices. Cook everything for 30 minutes.

CREAM OF BROCCOLI SOUP

1 package of chopped broccoli
½ cup of grated cheddar cheese
1 can of cream of mushroom soup
1 can of water
¼ teaspoon of thyme
Red pepper

Mix ingredients except cheese in a pot. Cover and simmer for 10 minutes. Add cheese and stir.

FRENCH ONION SOUP

4 large onions, thinly sliced
4 tablespoons margarine
10 ounces beef broth
½ cup dry sherry
2 teaspoons Worcestershire sauce
Pinch of pepper
French bread, thinly sliced
6 slices Swiss cheese
Parmesan cheese

Brown onion in margarine until tender. Add in beef broth, sherry, Worcestershire and pepper. Bring to a boil. In six individual bowls, pour the soup, float bread with slice of Swiss cheese on top. Sprinkle with Parmesan. Bake at 375 degrees for 15 to 20 minutes or under a broiler for 5 minutes.

HARBOR MASTER'S BEEF STEW

2 pounds of beef cut into 1-inch cubes
5 carrots cut into 1-inch slices
1 large onion, diced
3 stalks of celery, diced
1 quart of canned tomatoes or tomato juice
½ cup of quick cooking tapioca
½ teaspoon of ground clove
1 bay leaf
Salt and pepper to taste

Trim fat from beef. Put ingredients in a crock pot.
Cover and turn on high. Once it starts to cook, turn
to low and cook 4 to 5 hours. Remove bay leaf.

MINER'S STEW

1 pound of ground venison
2 celery stalks, chopped
3 potatoes, chopped
1 large carrot, diced
1 large can of tomato soup
1 small onion, chopped
½ teaspoon salt
½ teaspoon pepper
¼ teaspoon basil
¼ teaspoon rosemary
¼ teaspoon sage
1 tablespoon of flour mixed with
  2 tablespoons of water

Cook ground beef and onion in a skillet. Drain. In a large stew pan or pot, add beef, onion, tomato soup and 2 cans of water. Mix well. Add remaining ingredients. Cook on medium low heat until carrots and potatoes are soft. Add flour paste to thicken then stir.

JAMBALAYA

1 cup of raw oysters
  (or substitute cooked, cubed ham)
1 pound of raw shrimp, peeled and cleaned
½ cup of chopped green onion
½ cup of chopped white onion
1 green pepper cut into strips
½ cup of chopped celery
1 teaspoon of minced garlic
1/3 cup of butter
1 pound of canned tomatoes
1 cup of chicken broth
½ teaspoon of salt
½ teaspoon of cayenne pepper
1 cup of raw rice

In a pan or pot, sauté onion, green pepper, celery and garlic in butter until tender but not brown. Add shrimp and oysters and cook for five minutes. If you're using ham instead of oysters, add the ham with the rice. Add tomatoes, chicken broth, salt, cayenne and rice and stir then cover. Cook for 25 minutes over low heat or until rice is done. If mixture becomes dry, add a little tomato juice.

KITCHEN SINK GUMBO

2 pounds of shrimp in shells
1 pound of crab claws
1 pound of veal
1 pound of cubed ham
1 pound of chicken legs
2½ pounds of okra
3 tablespoons of cooking oil
1 large onion, diced
½ green pepper, diced
2½ quarts of water
2 tablespoons of chopped parsley
Cooked rice
Salt, pepper, paprika, garlic powder to taste

In a large pot, sauté onion and green pepper in 2 tablespoons of cooking oil. Add okra, cover and cook on low heat for 45 minutes. Shell shrimp and put the shells in a large container with 2½ quarts of water and bring to a boil. Strain and reserve liquid. In a large skillet with a tablespoon of oil, brown shrimp, veal, ham, parsley and chicken; seasoning with paprika, salt, pepper and garlic powder to taste. When okra has fried down, add all the meats and seasoning from skillet to okra the cover with reserved shrimp water. Cover and let simmer for 3 to 4 hours. 30 minutes before removing from the heat, add the crab claws. Serve over hot cooked rice.

VENISON

BARBECUED VENISON

3 pounds of venison
1 cup of ketchup
1 teaspoon of salt
2 teaspoons of Worcestershire sauce
¼ cup of vinegar
1 tablespoon of butter
½ teaspoon of cinnamon
3 slices of lemon
1 thinly sliced onion
1/8 teaspoon of allspice

Sear 3 pounds of venison in a skillet. Mix above ingredients in a saucepan and bring to a boil. Stir then simmer for 10 minutes. Cover venison with sauce and roast on a grill on in an oven at 350 degrees for 1½ to 2½ hours. Turn occasionally.

BREADED VENISON STEAK

4 venison steaks
1 egg
2 tablespoons of water
5 ounces of water
10 ounce can of cream of mushroom soup
1 cup of bread crumbs

Beat egg and water together. Dip the meat in the egg mixture and coat with bread crumbs. Brown meat in a skillet for 10 to 12 minutes on each side. Add mushroom soup into skillet with half a soup can of water. Simmer for 30 minutes or until you feel they are done to your taste.

BROWN SUGAR JERKY

5 pounds of venison
1¾ cups brown sugar
4 ounces of meat cure
3½ ounces soy sauce
3 tablespoons liquid smoke
5 cloves minced garlic

Cut meat into ¼ inch strips, removing fat. Combine ingredients in a plastic bag. Once mixed, put meat in bag and seal it. Place in fridge for 12 hours; knead every 2 to 3 hours. Remove meat from bag, wash and towel dry. Put on oven rack at low heat for 11 to 12 hours.

CHICKEN FRIED VENISON

2 pounds of venison steak (4 to 6 pieces)
1 beaten egg
¼ teaspoon garlic
¼ teaspoon onion salt
½ cup flour
1 cup cooking oil
Salt and pepper

Trim fat and membrane from meat. Pound steaks to tenderize and dip each piece in egg, followed by a mixture of garlic salt, onion salt and flour. Salt and pepper to taste and fry in cooking oil.

CITRUS GINGER DEER JERKY

2 pounds of venison steak
½ cup of soy sauce
2 tablespoons of lemon juice
1 teaspoon of ginger
¼ teaspoon of Tabasco sauce
1 teaspoon of liquid smoke
½ teaspoon of garlic salt
¼ teaspoon of pepper

Cut meat into thin, 1-inch strips and put in a bowl. Combine all ingredients thoroughly and pour over meat. Cover bowl and let stand for six hours. Lay strips on an oven rack with a cookie sheet beneath to catch the liquid. Bake at 175 degrees for 8 to 10 hours. Leave the oven door ajar slightly during baking.

DEER BURGERS

2 pounds of ground venison
5 tablespoons of Worcestershire sauce
2 eggs, beaten
25 Ritz crackers, crumbled

Crumble venison in a mixing bowl and add Worcestershire sauce. Leave in refrigerator for 30 minutes. Mix in beaten eggs and cracker crumbs. Form into burger size patties. Grill over medium heat or fry with a little oil.

DEER CAMP CHILI

3 small cans of kidney beans
4 small cans of crushed stewed tomatoes
8 garlic cloves, chopped
6 jalapenos with stems removed
  (3 diced without seeds)
1 red bell pepper, chopped
1 green bell pepper, chopped
1 pound of ground venison
1 pound of pork (or Italian sausage)
1 yellow onion, chopped
¼ bunch of cilantro
¾ tablespoon of oregano
¾ tablespoon of basil
¾ tablespoon of chili powder
1 tablespoon of salt
1 teaspoon of black pepper

Brown your meats of choice meat and drain. Add seasonings and vegetables and cook for 10 minutes on medium heat. Add tomatoes and beans, adjusting tomatoes to thin or thicken mixture. Cook until beans and vegetables are soft. The longer and slower the better tasting.

LEAVE IT ALONE VENISON STEW

1½ pounds of venison
1 cup of ginger ale
1 can of cream of mushroom soup
1 small can of mushrooms, chopped
1 package of dry onion soup mix

Mix all ingredients and pour into a tightly covered 9-inch by 12-inch baking dish. Bake at 350 degrees for 2½ to 3 hours. Resist peeking.

MARINATED VENISON STEAK

3 pounds of venison steak
1 onion, minced
1 tablespoon of vinegar
1 teaspoon of nutmeg
1 teaspoon of allspice
Flour
Salt and pepper
Water
Butter

Place meat in a glass baking dish. Combine onion, vinegar, nutmeg and allspice with enough water to cover the meat in the dish. Cover the dish and marinate in the refrigerator overnight. Stir occasionally. When it's time to cook, remove the meat from the marinade and salt, pepper and flour both sides. Fry steaks slowly in butter. For an extra kick use garlic butter or garlic salt.

OVEN RACK DEER JERKY

3 pounds of venison
2 teaspoons of onion powder
2 teaspoons of seasoning salt
2 teaspoons of Accent
½ teaspoon of pepper
½ teaspoon of garlic powder
½ cup of Worcestershire sauce
½ cup of soy sauce

Cut meat into ¼-inch thick slices. Combine all ingredients in a bowl and add meat. Marinate for 24 hours. Place meat slices on oven racks with foil underneath to catch any liquid. Bake at 150 degrees for 3 to 5 hours, longer if meat is not dried.

PAN BROILED VENISON

1 pound of venison steak
¼ pound of butter
Salt and pepper

Melt butter in a skillet and add venison steak. Broil one side until browned, about 5 minutes. Turn and brown the other side. Take off the heat and season with salt and pepper. Garlic salt works well too.

SLOPPY BUCK BBQ SANDWICHES

1 pound of ground venison
1 cup of water
½ cup of celery
1 tablespoon of mustard
1 tablespoon of ketchup
Celery seed or celery salt
4 ounces of chili sauce

Cook venison in a pan with water and celery until the celery is tender. Add in chili sauce, mustard, ketchup and celery seed/salt to taste. Simmer uncovered for 30 minutes. Serve on toasted hamburger buns.

VENISON CHOPS

6 venison chops
1 can of mushroom soup
Flour
Oil
Salt and pepper
Water

Dip chops in flour. In a pan, brown quickly in oil on both sides. Mix mushroom soup with 1 can of water and pour over chops. Simmer in the pan for 1 hour.

VENISON SAUSAGE CASSEROLE

1 pound of deer sausage
1 cup of celery, chopped
1 onion, chopped
1 cup of instant rice
1 package of onion soup mix
5 cups of water

Brown the sausage, celery and onion in a pan then drain the fat. Mix everything together in a baking dish. Bake at 350 degrees for 1 hour.

For more "Cookbooks for Guys" from author
Tim Murphy visit www.flanneljohn.com.

**FLANNEL JOHN'S
HUNTING & FISHING CAMP
COOKBOOK**
"A Good Meal Always Makes for a
Good Day"

**FLANNEL JOHN'S
WOODS & WATER
COOKBOOK**
"Critters, Fritters, Chili & Beer"

**FLANNEL JOHN'S
PIRATE GALLEY
COOKBOOK**
"Coastal Cuisine and Maritime Meals from
Oceans, Lakes & Rivers"

**FLANNEL JOHN'S
MOUNTAIN MAN
COOKBOOK**
"Frontier Food from the Hills, Country
and Backwoods"

FLANNEL JOHN'S
TAILGATING GRUB & COUCH POTATO
COOKBOOK
"Food for the Football Fanatic"

FLANNEL JOHN'S
SINGLE GUY COOKBOOK
"Simple Recipes with
Six Ingredients or Less"

FLANNEL JOHN'S
HEARTY BOWL COOKBOOK
"Soup, Stew, Chili & Chowder"

FLANNEL JOHN'S
HUNTING CABIN COOKBOOK
"Venison, Fowl & Wild Game"

THE TUBE STEAK BOOGIE COOKBOOK
"A Celebration of Hot Dogs, Brats,
Sausage & Kielbasa"

Made in the USA
Middletown, DE
20 October 2015